Original title:
Tying the Threads

Copyright © 2025 Creative Arts Management OÜ
All rights reserved.

Author: Robert Ashford
ISBN HARDBACK: 978-1-80586-057-0
ISBN PAPERBACK: 978-1-80586-529-2

Embroidered Echoes

In a world of tangled yarn,
Cats plot their cozy charms.
Needles dancing, oh so spry,
Stitching dreams as clouds float by.

Threads loop high and then they dip,
Every snip a comic trip.
Buttons laugh with all their might,
In this quilt of pure delight.

Knitted Kinship

Two grandmothers in a race,
Granny Smith gives a cheeky face.
They cast on stitches, swift and loud,
In this cozy, crafty crowd.

Yarn flies like a kite in spring,
Each purl a giggle, every sling.
Who knew socks could hold such glee?
In their hearts, they're young and free.

The Seamstress of Fate

She threads a needle with a wink,
Stitching truths and wine to drink.
Hemlines rise, and tales unfold,
With each loop, laughter gets bold.

Fabric sways like dancing feet,
While scissors prance to a funny beat.
Crafting chaos with a grin,
Who thought sewing could be this win?

Twined Aspirations

In a workshop filled with fluff,
Dreams are stitched, but it gets tough.
Patterns don't always match the plan,
But joy springs like a rubber band.

With every twist, a chuckle flows,
Who knew fiber had such prose?
We knit our hopes, we knit our fears,
And laugh together through the years.

Twists of Fate

In a world where socks go missing,
One shoe's lost while another's kissing.
A hat that dances on its own,
Must've eaten too much popcorn!

Life's a puzzle, pieces stray,
The cat chews yarn, leads them away.
Who knew a scarf could have such flair?
Or make a dog think it's a bear?

Interlaced Destinies

Two spaghetti strands collide at noon,
A pasta fight, oh, what a tune!
While meatballs giggle in delight,
Spinning tales through day and night.

A dance of threads, a wobbly waltz,
Where mismatched socks confess their faults.
The buttons pop and twirl about,
Each one holds secrets, no doubt!

Holding it All Together

Balloons float up, but one gets tangled,
In the crook of a tree, how it dangled!
A squirrel jumps, the party starts,
As confetti flies, it fills our hearts.

Glitter streams like winding paths,
While laughter echoes, chasing gaffes.
With every twist, a new surprise,
Who knew chaos could be such a prize?

The Yarn of Existence

Once there was a knitting bee,
Their honeyed thread was wild and free.
They spun a tale of joyous jest,
'Til the yarn unraveled at their fest.

A loop-de-loop of tangled fun,
As needles clink, the work is done.
But oh, beware the playful cat,
Who finds warm spots to sit and chat!

Threads of Legacy

In grandma's quilt, secrets hide,
Old stitches laugh, they can't abide.
Each patch a tale, a knotted jest,
In fabric fun, they feel the best.

Uncle Joe slipped, a yarn he spun,
Caught in a loop, oh what a run!
A legacy woven, bright and bold,
In every fold, a giggle told.

A Weave of Words

Words entwined like curly fries,
Silly phrases, oh what a prize!
Sentences twirl, a comical dance,
In laughter's grip, we take a chance.

Verb strings tied with silly flair,
Plot twists that tickle, beyond compare.
Rhymes knot up, a playful feat,
In this maze, we dare to meet.

Bound by Yarn

A ball of yarn rolls down the street,
Chasing the cat, now that's a treat!
Knots of chaos, giggles arise,
As tumbleweeds dance, in sunny skies.

Socks mismatched, a fashion quirk,
Tangled up in a playful work.
Stitches that bind have quite the cheer,
Crafting a tale that draws us near.

The Canvas of Emotion

Colors splash, emotions blend,
Each stroke a smile, every curve a bend.
A happy canvas, splattered bright,
Where laughter glows, and hearts take flight.

Paint drips down, a wobbly line,
Artistry born from ingredients fine.
In this gallery of joyous spree,
We sip our paint, and laugh with glee.

The Harmony of Hues

In a world where colors clash,
Red said to Blue, "You're such a brash!"
Yellow chimed in, all sunny and bright,
"Together we can cause quite a sight!"

Green rolled in with a cheeky grin,
"Let's mix it up, come join in,
A rainbow riot, let's paint the town,
Or maybe just wear a polka dot gown!"

Interlacing Lives

Once two folks, both quite the pair,
Met at a pub with silly hair.
"Let's grab a drink, mix it real nice!"
"I'll have a pint, you roll the dice!"

As stories flowed, so did the fun,
They laughed and danced, on the run.
"You're crazy!" one said with a cheer,
"This friendship's bound, let's drink another beer!"

The Stitched Narrative

A tailor sat with needle in hand,
Stitching up tales nobody planned.
"I'll patch your heart with laughter and glee,
Let's make a coat for you and me!"

With every thread, a story spun,
As buttons popped, such joy and fun.
"Who knew a seam could bring such delight?"
"Just don't wear it out on a laundry night!"

Echoes of the Loom

At the loom, the threads did dance,
Each twist and turn, a playful chance.
The weaver laughed, with a wink and a smile,
"Life's just a tapestry, stay for a while!"

Each knot held secrets, each weave a joke,
"Did you hear about the thread that spoke?"
"It said, 'I'm knot quite done with this spree!'
Join me, my friend, come weave with me!"

Woven Paths

In a land where socks go missing,
And shoes run off to play,
We've got a quest for laughter,
As fabric joins the fray.

With threads that twist and tangle,
A tapestry of cheer,
We sew our silly moments,
And stitch away our fear.

From buttons that keep hopping,
To zippers with a grin,
Our patchwork dreams are dancing,
Let the fun begin!

So grab your thread and needle,
And join our wacky quest,
Together we'll create our tale,
With laughter, we're the best!

Needle and Heart

A needle's in a pickle,
It pricks at every turn,
With hearts that laugh and giggle,
We end up with a burn.

We thread our silly stories,
Like yarn upon a loom,
Each stitch a joy, a worry,
Like flowers in a bloom.

With patches bright and funky,
We brighten every day,
Who knew this simple needle
Could lead us all astray?

So let's embrace our antics,
And dance beneath the sun,
For life's a crazy quilt,
Let's sew together fun!

Unraveling the Past

With yarn that tells a story,
Of patterns full of pride,
We knit our funny moments,
With puns we cannot hide.

The days are all a tangle,
With memories we share,
A knitted scarf of laughter,
With stories everywhere.

So slip upon those memories,
And wear them with a grin,
Each loop that holds our secrets,
Where chuckles can begin.

Let's unravel all the mishaps,
And stitch them back with cheer,
For every twist unstitches,
A giggle we hold dear!

The Seamstress's Touch

The seamstress cracks a smile,
With scissors in her hand,
She snips the threads of wonder,
And makes them dance and stand.

A patchwork of odd socks,
Decorates her bright room,
She chuckles at the chaos,
And sweeps away the gloom.

With every fold and tuck,
She weaves a tale so wild,
A fabric full of giggles,
Recalled from when she smiled.

So come, my quirky friends,
And join her crafty spree,
For in her seams of humor,
We find our laughter free!

Crossed Lines

In a world where wires cross,
I chased my cat, she's a boss.
She danced through yarn, oh what a sight,
A game of hide and seek at night.

Knots galore, like tangled hair,
I tried to fix it, pulled with care.
Yet every tug just made it worse,
My living room, a craft curse.

With laughter bubbling, I gave in,
Let chaos reign, let fun begin.
The tangled mess, a work of art,
My cat, the true creator's heart.

So here's to lines that twist and turn,
In every knot, there's love to learn.
Each giggle adds a brand new thread,
In silly messes, joy is bred.

Patterns of Affection

A quilt of hugs, so bold, so bright,
Each patch a joke, a sweet delight.
With polka dots and stripes galore,
We laugh together, who could ask for more?

In every layout, a tale untold,
Stitched up with love, pure and bold.
The pieced-up patterns show the way,
In goofy stories, we find our play.

From odd-shaped scraps, we build a dream,
Our laughter echoes like a happy stream.
Fuzzy edges, but perfectly true,
In every stitch, there's me and you.

So here's to patterns, wild and free,
In every twist, we find our glee.
Our fabric friendship, a vibrant blend,
Together stitched, we'll never end.

Interwoven Stories

In a land where threads collide,
Stories mingle, side by side.
A tale of socks that went astray,
One decided to take a holiday.

The mismatched pairs danced in the sun,
Two lonely socks having so much fun.
While I searched high and low for mates,
They staged a party, pulling pranks on plates.

With every tale that came to light,
Laughter echoed, pure delight.
The weave of life, though sometimes odd,
Brings joy in knots, thanks to our god.

So here's to stories, interlaced,
In every twist, our hearts embraced.
Though threads may tangle, we'll find a way,
To weave our fun in bright display.

The Stitch of Time

Seconds pass like fleeting thread,
In my sewing box, dreams are spread.
An hourglass spills with fabric flair,
I stitch my moments without a care.

With every tick, I sew and spin,
A thread of laughter, where to begin?
I patch the holes of days gone by,
Creating joy with a needle's sigh.

The clock may tick, but I must say,
I'd much prefer a yarn ballet.
For in my stitches, I find a rhyme,
A goofy dance to the beat of time.

So here's to moments, sewn with glee,
In every stitch, there's a memory.
As laughter spins the threads we wear,
A quilt of joy, forever rare.

The Yarn of Togetherness

In a world of tangled strings,
We laugh and dance in playful flings.
Socks that match? Not quite the case,
Yet here we are, a happy place.

We share a thread, a little joke,
A knitted cap, it makes us stoked.
Our mismatched mittens, quite the sight,
In cozy warmth, we feel just right.

Weaving Time

We stitch our days with goofy grace,
Each hour's fabric has a face.
From breakfast spills to coffee fights,
We weave our laughs in morning lights.

Our calendars, a patchwork grand,
Filled with mischief, oh so planned.
Each moment's thread, a silly tale,
In fun, we surely shall prevail.

A Quilt of Souls

A patch of moments, bright and bold,
Covering laughter, warmth, and gold.
Our crazy days, a crazy crew,
Stitched up tight with love so true.

In each square, a story lives,
With puns and hugs, the heart it gives.
Our quilt of souls, it keeps us warm,
Through windy storms, we huddle, charm.

Sewn with Intent

With needle sharp and fabric fine,
We sew our lives, oh so divine.
A stitch of laughter, a dash of cheer,
In every seam, our bond is clear.

We patch the days for fun and bliss,
Finding humor in each miss.
Our laughter threads all through the night,
In every loop, there's pure delight.

Stitching Memories

In Grandma's quilt, I found a sock,
A relic lost in time's great clock.
Each patch a tale, a laugh to share,
Where mismatched stitches show we care.

The dog ran off with Dad's old hat,
Now it's a pillow for the cat.
With every rip, a story's born,
Of frayed edges, laughter never worn.

A youth spent chasing errant seams,
In every stitch, there lived our dreams.
We thread our lives, both wild and free,
In every knot, pure comedy.

So here's to fibers, tightly spun,
A fabric of memories, all in fun.
As we patch the holes, let laughter rise,
In every stitch, love never dies.

Knots of Affection

A shoelace tangled 'neath my chair,
Caused quite a ruckus, I do declare.
With every tug, it gave a fight,
I laughed so hard, lost track of night.

Socks that vanish, what a mess,
In the dryer, they dance and dress.
When I pair them up, it's quite a sight,
Funky friends in mismatched light!

My buddy's beard caught in a snare,
A thread of yarn, oh, what a scare!
He swayed and spun like a wild fool,
Turns out, humor's the greatest tool.

In every knot, a loving grin,
Life's little tangles, let's dive in.
We laugh at frays, and all that bends,
For in each knot, pure joy extends.

The Cosmic Loom

Stars are woven in the sky,
A cosmic dance, oh me, oh my!
Planets spinning, threads of night,
Even comets join the flight.

Aliens giggle as they weave,
In a fabric of dreams, they believe.
Galactic yarn wrapped 'round a tree,
What a sight, don't you agree?

Black holes gulp and take a snack,
As space-time unwinds, no looking back.
Each twist and twirl, a grand display,
The universe has a funny way.

So catch a comet, if you can,
Join the fun, be part of the plan.
In the cosmic loom, we all belong,
Stitching together, a joyful song.

Interlaced Journeys

Two trains crossed on a map so grand,
Mismatched tracks, what a comedy band!
With every clang, a hearty cheer,
Who knows where we'll end up, dear?

Road trips tangled in a snack attack,
With crumbs and giggles, there's no lack.
Lost my way, but what's the fuss?
Every wrong turn's a joyous plus!

Bicycle rides, oh what a scene,
Pedals tangled, but we're still keen.
With laughter echoing through the park,
Our journey shines bright, a joyful spark.

So let's embrace the turns we take,
With humor woven in every break.
Interlaced paths, we all can roam,
In this tangled life, we find our home.

One Fabric, Many Colors

In a patchwork world, we all stand,
Sewing wild dreams with a clumsy hand.
The reds laugh loud, the blues chase around,
Together we dance, where mishaps abound.

Stitches might wobble and seams may fray,
But who needs perfection, come out and play?
With laughter so bright, we bask in the hue,
One fabric, many colors, just me and you.

So grab your scissors, let's cut and weave,
In our own chaos, there's joy to retrieve.
A plaid of mishmash, a quilt that's our fate,
In this colorful mess, we all celebrate.

Let's patch it up with a grin and a wink,
Life's like a canvas, or so I think.
With every bright yarn, the laughter will grow,
Together spun tales, like a comedy show.

Lace and Legacy

Lace so delicate, a sight to behold,
We tangled our moments, both smooth and bold.
With frills and with flops, we danced without care,
A legacy woven, with quirks we all share.

The grandma's old lace, it's frayed at the edges,
But don't you dare ask, she'll raise all the ledges!
"Just a little nip here, a tuck on the side,"
She stitches her secrets, with laughter and pride.

A runner on tables and quite on the floor,
It holds all the tales of the family lore.
From weddings to teardrops, the memories nest,
In lace and in laughter, we've truly been blessed.

So gather around, with a cup and a cheer,
For legacies soft, that we hold so dear.
In fabric so fine, our stories connect,
With humor and love, what more could we expect?

The Thread of Understanding

A thread that wanders, gets lost, then returns,
Through laughter and mishaps, it twists and it churns.
We can't quite agree on the color or hue,
But somehow in chaos, we find something new.

One says it's azure, another insists gold,
While others are laughing, a sight to behold.
But in the perplexing hues of our fate,
We learn that acceptance is never too late.

Through knots and through tangles, we smile and we nod,
For every strange fabric's a little like God.
The truth's in the laughter that rises with glee,
As we share in the journey, just you and me.

So let's hold the yarn and unravel the tales,
In conversations where humor prevails.
A thread that connects us, it's stitched with a grin,
In this woven caper, together we win!

Held Together

In a world like a quilt, with patches galore,
We stitch up our memories and keep wanting more.
With mismatched buttons and zippers that squeak,
We giggle and chuckle at every small tweak.

The sleeves that don't fit and the pockets that flop,
In life's crazy fabric, we gather and hop.
Though seams may be loose and be fraying today,
Together we tackle, we laugh all the way.

Let's gather our quirks, and hold them like treasure,
Each odd little piece brings unmeasured pleasure.
From socks that don't match to spoons in the stew,
With laughter our glue, we're never askew.

So here's to the chaos that keeps us in sync,
With every odd stitch, we find a new link.
In the fabric of life, let's cherish the blend,
For the fun in the weaving will never quite end!

Knitted Patterns

In a world of yarn and needles,
A cat thinks it's a jungle
Pouncing through the knitted fields,
Chasing that rogue ball of fun.

Laughter echoes as we stitch,
Mistakes become cozy quirks,
A scarf that's more like a twist,
Who knew crafting could be a stunt?

Grandma's patterns start to fray,
Her cat's decided to assist,
Swirls and fluffs become the game,
Yarn bombs fly, a wild twist!

With jelly beans as our treat,
We knit until the night's complete,
In a chaos of threads and glee,
Our hearts, like blankets, warm and free.

Weaving the Unseen

Invisible threads weave our tales,
Through whispers and giggles, it sails,
Each secret knot a funny plot,
A friendship that always prevails.

Spools of laughter roll away,
Caught in a tangle, we play,
With every twist, we share a joke,
Our bond grows stronger day by day.

Invisible looms make us dance,
A grand parade in our own pants,
With each silly move, we collide,
Bright colors blend in this strange romance.

So here we are, mischief in tow,
As we loop and twist for the show,
Our unseen threads vibrate with joy,
In the fabric of life, we freely grow.

Fabric of the Soul

Woven with care, our silly ways,
Patchworked memories, bright displays,
A fabric that giggles and sighs,
As we bumble through our crazy days.

Each thread a story, some old, some new,
With a dash of rhinestones and glue,
We're stitching a quilt of our dreams,
And a sock that's lost, oh, two!

Twisted fibers stand up and dance,
While we giggle at a chance,
To wear mismatched socks—what a style!
In this fabric, we find our romance.

So grab some threads, let's make it bright,
Mufflers and mittens, a silly sight,
We'll wrap our souls in laughter's grace,
And weave together with delight.

The Spiral of Affection

Round and round, the yarn does go,
A spiral of joy, a crafty show,
With each loop, a hug is drawn,
In threads of laughter, we flow.

Spinning tales like fibers entwined,
With puns that are silly, not maligned,
A twist here, a giggle there,
Our hearts are stitched, perfectly aligned.

Knots of kindness vs. tangle of woe,
We laugh at the chaos, as we bestow,
Quirky gifts wrapped in jingles,
As love and mischief brightly glow.

So gather 'round with laughter and cheer,
In our spiral of fun, we hold dear,
With each twist and giggle, we find,
Life's tapestry is best when it's clear.

The Web of Us

In a land where socks all go to hide,
We find each other, step aside!
Mismatched shoes, a kaleidoscope,
Together we dance, we intertwine hope.

Like spaghetti on a first date night,
Twisted and tangled, but oh what a sight!
Laughter erupts from each silly snag,
In our wobbly waltz, we happily brag.

We twirl around with a cheerful cheer,
Every clumsy fall brings us near.
In our knitted chaos, love's the thread,
Even when one of us bumps our head!

So let's embrace the mess we create,
With yarns of joy, we celebrate.
Through giggles and knots, our bond will fuss,
In this wild web, forever it's us!

A Cord of Compassion

Two shoelaces stretched across the town,
We trip and stumble, but never frown.
One pulls you up, the other holds tight,
In a silliness dance, we find delight.

A rubber band flinging with such flair,
Snapping friendships here and there.
We stretch our jokes with a twang and a snap,
Together we bounce in a colorful map!

Like silly putty, we mold and we play,
Creating laughter to brighten the day.
Our hearts are stitched with laughter and care,
A goofy patchwork we gladly share.

So let's wrap ourselves in giggles and jest,
With our silly bonds, we're truly blessed.
In the dance of life, we're each other's grace,
Together forever, at a joyful pace!

Shadows and Stitches

In the patchwork quilt of life so bright,
We're shadows and stitches, a curious sight.
A needle that dances, a thimble that sings,
Every poke of laughter, a warmth it brings.

Tangled up stories, with threads of fun,
Jumping like bunnies, oh snap—did we run?
Spools of yarn unravel our silly schemes,
Twirling through days, lost in our dreams.

Buttons that pop like the jokes we share,
Wobbling along, we haven't a care.
We trip on our words, but who's keeping score?
With stitches of humor, we'll always want more!

So let's wield our scissors with giggling glee,
Cutting through troubles, wild and free.
In this tapestry, we'll find our groove,
Together in shadows, with laughter we move!

Embraced by Fabric

In a closet of chaos, we twirl and spin,
Fabric friendship, where adventures begin.
Like a quirky quilt made with mismatched flair,
We wrap our worries, a bond beyond compare.

A ribbon of laughter, we knot and we tie,
With a sprinkle of joy as the days flutter by.
Draped in the charm of our silly schemes,
We sail through the fabric of friendship dreams!

Stitches of giggles, we sew on each day,
Every seam holds stories, come what may.
With patches of humor, we cover each fall,
In this cozy embrace, we welcome it all!

So let's thread our hearts with laughter's delight,
In a world of fabric, we'll shine so bright.
No fray can untangle this merry embrace,
Together we bloom, in our fabulous space!

Weaving Whispers

In a room where snickers brew,
Strings of laughter twirl and skew,
Grandma's yarn, it goes awry,
Neighbors peek and wonder why.

Kittens pounce on woolly balls,
Their antics echo off the walls,
We dodge the chaos with a grin,
A tangled mess we call our kin.

Threads entwined like gossip flies,
A fabric made of clever lies,
With every stitch, a chuckle shared,
In this quilt, absurdity's spared.

At the end, we stand with glee,
A masterpiece of jubilee,
So let the laughter intertwine,
In our wacky, wooly design!

Bound by the Loom

At the loom, we dance and play,
Tangled tales in bright arrays,
Friends in stitches, who'd have thought?
Creating chaos, all for naught!

With threadbare jokes, we weave a cheer,
Creating giggles, never fear,
Missteps lead to laughter loud,
In this workshop, we're all proud.

Measuring smiles in yards of fun,
Everyone gets to join the run,
A fraying edge, but hearts are tight,
In clumsy knots, we'll take our flight.

The loom may break, but we won't mind,
Our eccentric fabric will unwind,
For in this mess, we make our home,
Tales of joy wherever we roam!

Stitched in Silence

A needle's dance with silent grace,
Whispers echo in this space,
Yet every stitch, a secret told,
In quiet corners, we're twofold.

Threading needle, oh what fun,
Our playful jabs, a sneaky pun,
With every loop, a laugh is trapped,
In our cocoon, the humor's wrapped.

Each patch we make, a tale so sly,
Under the radar, we reach for the sky,
With zipper mouths and twinkling eyes,
A soft convention of sweet goodbyes.

As laughter threads its way around,
In silence, joy is gently found,
So let our quirks and quirks unite,
In stitched-up giggles, we take flight!

The Fabric of Us

A quilt of quirks, oh what a sight,
Every pattern makes it bright,
With crazy motifs and colors wild,
We stitch together like a child.

Funky prints and mismatched seams,
Patchwork laughter fills our dreams,
In every block, a joke resides,
Through fabric bonds, our joy abides.

We measure friendship in cozy rows,
With playful tales that come and go,
As needles jab, the humor flows,
Embracing chaos, nothing slows.

So raise a toast to what we make,
This zany cloth, in every quake,
Together, stitched in humor's hue,
The fabric of us, bright and new!

Knotting Dreams

In dreams I find a tangled bait,
Loops and knots at every rate.
My socks refuse to play along,
They dance in pairs and sing a song.

I tried to weave a grand design,
But all I made was quite a line.
The yarn rolled away with glee,
Leaving a puzzle just for me.

Woolly creatures make a fuss,
When I declare my knitting bust.
They snicker from the cozy chair,
Claiming all I do is tear.

Yet laughter fills the knotted air,
With gags and laughter everywhere.
For in this mess, I've found my cheer,
Joining the colors, year by year.

Interwoven Journeys

On every path, there's thread to tread,
I step with shoes that have misread.
Adventures twist, unspool, and sprain,
I laugh as I trip on magical chain.

My friends, they giggle, wagging tongues,
As I weave tales with silly songs.
The maps we made are far from straight,
But who needs rules? We just create.

In every stitch, a story grows,
From spaghetti trips to lost toes.
Our fabric's vibrant, never dull,
In this chaotic, colorful hull.

Together we sew the silly seams,
Life unravels, rippling dreams.
With laughter stitched into our hearts,
We're artful messes, funny parts.

The Connective Stitch

I found a string while on a climb,
It led to giggles, bells, and chime.
I tugged on it—oh, what a blast!
A kitten popped up, what a cast!

The thread followed me on a merry chase,
To pizza places and silly face.
Each pull, a surprise, a pie in the air,
Who knew yarn would laugh and share?

I thought I'd knit a lovely rise,
Instead, I wore a scarf of pies.
My grandma chuckled, "What a sight!
Your fashion sense is pure delight!"

So let it weave and let it twirl,
A funny yarn that makes you whirl.
In every loop, there's joy and jest,
Connected threads, we laugh the best!

Boundless Fibers

With every fiber, I make a joke,
A puppet show made of soft wool stoke.
The fibers giggle as I weave,
Creating gifts that make you leave.

A hat with eyes, a scarf for paws,
I win the day, I earn applause.
But every time my needle breaks,
It starts a dance that oddly shakes.

I frantically chase the rolling thread,
Hoping it won't end up dead.
My pets are laughing, what a sight,
Chasing fibers, left and right.

Yet in this chaos, joy prevails,
With every knot, a thousand tales.
Boundless fibers, what a treat,
Life's a stitch, and oh so sweet!

The Art of Connection

Two clowns met at a party, oh my!
One with a tie, the other a pie.
They danced in circles, laughing aloud,
A friendship bloomed, under a cloud.

They drew their maps on napkins so grand,
One with a fork, the other with a hand.
They plotted their travels on jelly and jam,
With giggles and chuckles, they hatched a plan.

Through fences they leaped, through puddles they sped,
With pants full of mud, they were joyfully wed.
The world was their stage, eccentric and bright,
In a circus of antics, they danced through the night.

Balloons and confetti soared high in the air,
Each twist and turn was a venture to share.
In the art of connection, they painted with glee,
Two jesters united, in their own jubilee.

Fabricated Affection

A cat and a dog, what a curious pair,
One loved to meow, the other to stare.
They hatched a grand scheme, to share a big bone,
But each thought the other would prefer it alone.

They tried to play fetch, but it turned into fun,
The dog brought the stick, the cat brought a bun.
As they laughed and they rolled, they learned in a flash,
That friendship could grow from a humorous clash.

With yarn balls and socks, they crafted a game,
A tug-of-war battle, oh what a fame!
With antics so silly, their joy was contagious,
In a world made of fluff, it felt quite outrageous.

Fabricated affection, though funny at best,
Grew sturdier bonds, like a comfy nest.
For laughter and quirks tied them up with delight,
A cat and a dog, what a marvelous sight!

Woven Whispers

In a room full of yarn, a gathering sprang,
Where grandmas and grandpas began to bang.
Knitting together, their secrets did flow,
With whispers of gossip and mischievous glow.

They crafted a blanket, so cozy and wide,
With stitches of laughter, they set aside pride.
Each loop held a story, each knot had a jest,
Making memories in stitches, they felt truly blessed.

They spun tales of youth, of love and a fall,
Of how they once danced at the biggest ball.
As yarn tangled up, their hearts did unite,
For woven whispers lit up through the night.

With furrows and fumbles, they cherished the knack,
In every mistake, there was no way to slack.
From laughter to yarn, their threads intertwined,
Creating a tapestry, perfectly aligned.

The Fabric of Connection

There once was a tailor who fancied a seam,
Sewed up a suit, not as sweet as a dream.
With pockets too big and sleeves like a spoon,
He laughed at the fashion, it felt far too soon.

His friend brought a shirt, mismatched and loud,
Together they strutted, feeling quite proud.
In patterns that clashed, their laughter erupted,
A duo so silly, it simply corrupted.

With buttons that wobbled and zippers that stuck,
They tumbled through life, like a curious luck.
In the fabric of connection, they stitched their own way,
Making blunders and thrumbles, come what may.

So if you find clothes that don't quite fit right,
Remember the tailor and his friend's silly plight.
In laughter and threads, they wove a fine tale,
For joy is the fabric that'll always prevail.

Echoes of Entanglement

I grabbed the yarn with great delight,
But it danced away, just out of sight.
My cat's a pro at sabotage,
Knocking my project without a pause.

With needles clattering like some jam,
I tried to stitch, but got a slam!
The coffee spilled, the colors blend,
I'd call it art if I had a friend.

Stitched with Care

Sewed a patch that's shaped like cheese,
My shirt now smells like mice and peas.
I thought I'd mend it, make it swell,
But now it's thrift shop material, oh well!

My friends all laugh, my ego's sore,
They say I should stick to crafts no more.
But here I am with needle and thread,
Creating laughter, not fear or dread.

Knitting the Soul

With each knit, a giggle sewn,
I tangled up in chaos grown.
The pattern chart, a cryptic foe,
One stitch forward, three stitches to go.

My project grows, a creature bizarre,
Is it a blanket, or a drumming guitar?
I wear it proud on my head like a crown,
The fashion police? They'll never come 'round!

Threads of Time

As I weave through the days like a fine old knit,
I find missing patterns; not a single bit.
Time's slipped through, it has a knack,
I'll knit it back, or take a snack!

So here's to twists and loops gone awry,
I'll dance with colors, let laughter fly.
For in the end, it's all just a jest,
My tangled heart feels truly blessed.

Threads of Destiny

In a closet bright, socks take flight,
Lost to the depths, a curious sight.
A lonely pair hops, won't reunite,
While one socks dances, oh what a plight!

Buttons roll wild, they form a band,
With a sock puppet show, quite unplanned.
They laugh and they tumble, all at hand,
In this world of fabric, chaos is grand!

Stray threads wander, in patterns unknown,
Trying to weave a story of their own.
But loops and knots turn to folly grown,
As they snicker and tease, they're never alone!

Oh, the fabric of life, a patchwork dream,
With every mistake, it's not as it seems.
A snip here, a cut there, it bursts at the seams,
In this silly adventure, we're all on the beams!

The Needle's Dance

On a table bright, buttons spin 'round,
While the needle prances, there's joy to be found.
Threading its way, with a playful bound,
It jiggles and wobbles, a joyful sound!

Sequins shine bright, like stars in a line,
Joining the party, everyone's fine.
Stitching and glitching, a crafty design,
With a wink and a nod, they sip on some wine!

Patches are shouting, 'We're all the same!'
Yet each has a story, with fabric to claim.
While zippers are zipping, and velcro's to blame,
For sticking together, this world is a game!

Oh, what a dance, in a quilted embrace,
Where fabric friends gather, each with their place.
In the merry confusion, a smile on each face,
Let's stitch up our laughter, at a jubilant pace!

Strands of Existence

In the drawer of life, all tangled and neat,
Strands of existence, oh what a feat!
They twist and they twirl, on this crazy street,
Dancing to rhythms, they can't help but cheat!

Yarn balls are giggling, oh what a mess,
Knots in the system, oh, they do impress!
With a flick of the wrist, they shout, 'Non-stress!'
These threads of laughter, they simply bless!

Now a ribbon winds up, ready to fly,
While twine and string whisper, 'Don't be shy!'
In this yarn ball world, you laugh till you cry,
As stitches and seams wink, they wave you goodbye!

So gather your threads and make something swell,
With humor and joy, they weave tales to tell.
In the tapestry of life, let laughter propel,
For every forgotten knot, there's a story to sell!

Fraying Edges

Fraying edges dance, like wild little sprites,
Laughing and tugging through fabric-filled nights.
A seam's coming loose, much to our delights,
While the thread pulls its pranks, causing silly fights!

Old clothes have stories, with rips and with tears,
Each thread a memory, oh, who really cares?
With patches of laughter, they slip through the snares,
Creating a fabric that giggles and dares!

Oh, buttons are falling, they can't take the heat,
While zippers and snaps try to admit defeat.
Yet with playful antics, they answer the beat,
In this world of garments, you'll never feel beat!

So embrace those frays, with whimsy and cheer,
For every loose thread tells a story so dear.
In the tapestry life spins, we draw nearer,
To the joy of our chaos, let's make that clear!

A Patchwork of Moments

In the cupboard, scraps are found,
Some are funny, some profound.
Stitches here and stitches there,
A quilt of laughs beyond compare.

My cat thinks it's all for him,
He lounges, dreams, and makes a whim.
With every patch, a giggle grows,
As I recount my crafty woes.

Buttons bouncing, threads that fray,
Lost my needle, where'd it play?
Socks in pairs sure look fine,
But one went rogue, just to dine!

Together we laugh, mine and yours,
In swirls of color, joy ensures.
Crafting memories, what a blend,
A patchwork life that has no end.

Knots in Time

In the attic, knots I find,
Each tied with laughter, sweetly blind.
Grandma's yarn has yarns to tell,
With each loop, it casts a spell.

My dog thinks it's a tug-of-war,
Pulling threads right out the door.
Oh dear, what a playful mess,
These knots of joy, I must confess!

Time weaves in with glee and grace,
Laughter echoes, a friendly race.
As I fumble, chuckles rise,
A comical dance with no goodbyes.

You tie a knot, I tie the shoe,
As friends we bond with something new.
Lifetimes mixed, we try and climb,
Caught in giggles, knots in time.

Embroidery of Experience

With needle poised, I take a shot,
Stitching tales, a colorful plot.
Each thread's a laugh, a moment spun,
In every loop, there's giggles run.

Textures clash, a vibrant spree,
My fabric dance, a wild jubilee!
Mismatched patterns, oh so bright,
In this canvas, we take flight.

Oops, I spilled coffee on my art,
"Coffee stain chic," I start to impart.
Bobbin dancing, what a sight,
As threads unravel, sheer delight.

In stitches woven, joy abounds,
With every tug, pure fun surrounds.
Together we craft, but always cheer,
An embroidery of hearts, forever dear.

Wrapped in Connection

Gather 'round, let's weave a tale,
Of threads we share, they never pale.
Your yarn is bright, mine's a bit shy,
Together we laugh, oh my, oh my!

In the park, a tangle so sly,
Jumping ropes that touch the sky.
Hiccups happen, so do falls,
Life's silly moments that enthrall.

Twirling like ribbons, we dance and sway,
Woven in friendship, come what may.
With every turn, a chuckle appears,
Wrapped in connection over the years.

So grab your yarn and bring your fun,
For crafting joy has just begun.
In colors bright, let laughter sing,
Wrapped in connection, our hearts take wing.

Fabrics of the Heart

In a world made of fabric, we laugh and we play,
Stitches of joy stitch the blues all away.
Socks in the dryer, they're running amok,
A game of hide and seek, oh what a shock!

Quilted in laughter, we dance and we spin,
Each patch tells a story, let the fun begin!
A scarf tells a secret, a hat holds a grin,
Together we're silly, through thick and through thin.

Fabrics unravel, but our spirits don't fray,
Those messy seams remind us to stay.
With threads made of giggles, we weave through the strife,
A patchwork of joy, it's the fabric of life!

So let's twirl and twist, let our stitches unite,
In this comedy of fabrics, everything feels right!
From buttons to zippers, they all play their part,
In this quilt of the world, we sew from the heart!

Bound by Threads

In a world full of knots, we find such delight,
Like spaghetti on Tuesday, it's quite a sight!
With yarn balls bouncing, and kites in the air,
We stitch up the laughter, with giggles to share.

Tangled together, we're pals through it all,
Like socks with a hole, we just can't let fall.
A patch on the elbow, a smile on the face,
In the fabric of friendship, there's always a space.

With every little hiccup, we mend and we patch,
Our threads may be fraying, but there's not a catch.
In a blanket of giggles, we snuggle up tight,
Bound by our spirit, we shine like the light.

So grab a loose thread, let's dance and let's twine,
In this vast tapestry, oh isn't it fine!
From buttons to patches, it's all quite absurd,
Bound by our laughter, not a single word.

Fiber of Unity

In the loom of the world, we weave side by side,
With colors of laughter, it's such a wild ride!
Each fiber a friend, each thread is a tale,
When we stitch up the fun, we will surely prevail.

They say life's a fabric, but we make it a joke,
With puns and some stitching, our joy's never broke.
Let's knot up our worries, let's knit up some fun,
In the fabric of unity, we all are as one.

A quilt made of smiles, a patch full of cheer,
Threads sewn with laughter are something we steer.
With a needle of kindness, we mend every tear,
In this grand tapestry, there's love everywhere!

So roll with the thread, let your spirits unwind,
In this fabric of fortune, our joys all entwined.
With fiber of unity, we craft and create,
A world full of giggles, oh isn't it great!

The Golden Stitch

In the tapestry of life, a golden thread gleams,
With a wink and a nod, it supports all our dreams.
Sewing on laughter, trimming off fears,
It binds us together, through smiles and through tears.

With buttons of kindness and zippers of care,
We stitch every moment, our joy we will share.
From patchwork adventures, we spin and we play,
In this quilt of existence, we brighten each day.

A golden stitch here, a twirl over there,
Through the blunders and giggles, we still make our flair.
In this woven adventure, we each have a role,
With laughter as thread, oh it brightens the soul!

So let's gather our fibers and dance through the seams,
With a golden thread shining bright in our dreams.
In this cloth of our lives, may the fun never cease,
With stitches of joy, we find our sweet peace!

Knots of Kindness

In a world of tangled yarn,
Cats think it's a game to play,
Chasing tails and curling dreams,
As laughter echoes through the fray.

Grandma's knitting, what a sight,
Pulling loops with all her might,
But every stitch comes loose with glee,
A scarf that's really one long sneeze!

Friends gather 'round with needles high,
Creating chaos, oh my, oh my!
One scarf turns to five, it's true,
We laugh, we spill, and sometimes stew!

Each knot a memory, all in jest,
In this silly crafting fest,
For every slip and silly twirl,
We weave the threads of our world.

Strands of Solitude

Alone in a room with wool in hand,
A battle against knots, it's unplanned,
Every loop's a riddle, can't find the end,
Seems solitude loves to play pretend.

Talking to yarn, oh what a plight,
It rolls away, it's quite a fright,
"Let's be friends!" I cry in vain,
"Stop acting like you're on a train!"

I trip on hardly anything, oh dear,
My ball of yarn goes flying near,
Bouncing off walls, what a surprise,
Who knew solitude wore such disguise?

Yet in this tangle, joy I weave,
With every mishap, I just believe,
That even in chaos, laughter's found,
In every strand, a bit of joy is bound.

Embrace of the Tapestry

Woven dreams and crazy seams,
We pull each yarn with childish schemes,
At the loom where laughter flows,
We create a masterpiece from woes.

Oh, the patterns are quite absurd,
A cat, a dog, and flying bird,
We quilt our life with laughter bright,
What's wrong with a polka dot fright?

In the tapestry, faces gleam,
Each patch a memory, or so it seems,
But one too many, oh what a twist,
Now it's just a colorful mist!

Yet every thread, in silliness tied,
With friends around, I can't abide,
For in this weave, joy's the key,
Together we'll make history!

The Invisible Bond

Strange things happen, we can't quite see,
Like two left socks in a laundry spree,
A friend to share, to laugh, and jest,
In this silly game, we're truly blessed.

Invisible threads, oh where do they go?
Like lost marbles in a circus show,
We chase each other round the bend,
Hoping to catch the next big trend!

At first, we link like a pinky swear,
But then we trip, and who can care?
Laughter erupts—the perfect guide,
In this invisible bond, we abide.

So let's make messes, let's have our fun,
Twisting and turning, we won't be done,
For every laugh, for every gaffe,
In our hearts, the sweetest laugh!

Threads of Connection

In a world full of knots, we giggle and gloat,
As connections are made with a noodle and boat.
Silly old socks, they wander and roam,
Finding their partners to make a new home.

A cat with a yarn ball, oh what a sight,
Rolling and tumbling, it gives us delight.
Unraveling tales that make grandmas snort,
Who knew a loose thread would start such a sport?

Tangled in laughter, we trip and we fall,
Witty young kids with their makeshift wall.
A blanket of chuckles, we gather and weave,
In this merry mess, there's nothing to leave.

So spin us a yarn, let the humor take flight,
With mismatched apparel, we dance through the night.
Every goof and a twist, a treasure to keep,
In this merry tapestry, we dive in so deep.

Lattice of Lives

In the web of our days, we zig and we zag,
While grandpa's odd jokes make us laugh till we sag.
Mom's cooking up chaos, oh what a delight,
Her burnt soufflé takes off like a kite!

Bouncing off walls like a ball made of cheese,
We float through our lives, doing just as we please.
A neighborly wink, a mad dash to the store,
Somehow we land with our heads on the floor.

We sew up adventures with giggles and glee,
Each awkward encounter a part of the spree.
Who knew that our lives would be such a show?
With sacrifices made for that last slice of dough?

So we pluck at the strings, making music of cheer,
With wild stories shared over mugs of cold beer.
Through the silly missteps and slips that we take,
We laugh as we weave our sublime little cake.

Fabric of Memories

Stitching together each zany escapade,
With memories woven that never do fade.
Like grandma's old quilt with the patches so bright,
Every square has a tale that brings pure delight.

In the mess of our laughter, we find a warm place,
With ink on our fingers and crumbs on our face.
A family of goofs on a grand mission,
Our fabric unravels through love and ambition.

As time threads its needle, we dance down the lane,
Adventurous hearts while we drip with the rain.
We tumble together, with mismatched attire,
A cacophony woven, a comedic choir.

So here's to the weave, the colorful swirl,
To moments that sparkle in this quirky world.
With stitches of joy in each day that we pen,
We'll gather our threads and do it again!

Weft and Warp

In the loom of our lives, we tangle and twist,
With shenanigans woven in every sweet kiss.
Mom's baking a cake, it turns into a race,
With frosting like paint on our faces, a base!

Let's hop on a thread, take a ride on a shoe,
As we bounce through the strands of our colorful crew.
A squirrel with a hat is the star of the show,
As we laugh at the sight—oh where did it go?

We hurtle through mazes of yarn and of lace,
Inventing our games with a quirky embrace.
Through the tangled mess, there's a sparkle of cheer,
Each slip-up we make, oh how grand it appears!

So gather your threads, bring the laughter alive,
In a world of our making, where all can survive.
With jokes tightly woven, let friendship ignite,
In the fabric of joy, we find our delight!

Weaving Through Life

In a room full of spools, oh so bright,
I tripped on a package, what a sight!
Threads tangled with laughter, made a mess,
Who knew chaos could be such a success?

My cat thought the yarn was a snack,
Chasing and pouncing, no skill to lack.
I yelled, 'That's not dinner, you silly thing!'
But in her eyes, I saw joy take wing.

A patchwork of moments, all intertwined,
Each clumsy mistake, a treasure to find.
We stitch up our lives with giggles and quirks,
And love's the fabric, where every heart lurks.

So let's raise a toast to this colorful ride,
Where laughter and threads take us far and wide.
With needles of humor, we sew ever tight,
In this crazy quilt called life, oh what a sight!

The Art of Connection

Two dogs with a leash—what a site to behold,
Tangled like spaghetti, quite a story to be told.
They sniff and they bark, in a chaotic ballet,
While their owners both chuckle, trying to sway.

A coffee date turned disaster—my cup's in the air,
Splashed on his shirt, but I didn't care.
'It's like abstract art!' I blurted with glee,
He laughed and replied, 'You're such a mess, you see!'

Emails went missing, I hit 'reply all' too,
My cat memes went viral, who knew it's true?
In the art of connection, we fumble and fall,
Yet these little moments surround us like a wall.

So let's keep it messy, let's keep it real,
We'll gather our laughs like a delicious meal.
For in every blunder, a bond grows anew,
With giggles as glue, we'll stick like glue!

Delicate Bonds

A kite in the breeze, oh what a show,
I lost my grip on it—oh no, oh no!
It soared with a laugh and danced with delight,
While I stood there waving, what a silly sight!

Friendship like feathers, soft yet so strong,
In the wind, we may wobble, but we can't be wrong.
With a wink and a chuckle, we float through the air,
Sometimes we crash down, but, hey, we don't care!

A slip on a banana, oh how I fell,
But the laughter that followed rang like a bell.
We gather our moments, both big and so small,
In delicate bonds, we just have a ball.

So let's twirl like ribbons in the summer breeze,
Embracing our awkwardness, if you please.
With smiles as our anchors, we'll stick through the waves,

In this crazy merry-go-round, oh how our heart craves!

Twisted Histories

Once upon a time, I tried to be neat,
With ribbons and bows, I couldn't face defeat.
I tied one too tight and got stuck on a chair,
The laughter erupted, a delightful affair.

Grandma's knitting lesson led me astray,
Turns out, her wisdom was tied in a way.
'You knit through life, don't take it too hard,'
But I tangled my yarn like a bard in my yard.

Unraveling stories, wrapped up in our dreams,
With giggles and grumbles, life's bursting at seams.
We weave our own myths, no need to be dull,
In a tapestry woven with laughter, so full.

So let's mix up our threads, our legends askew,
With joy as our compass, life's a zoo—who knew?
In the grand scheme of things, we won't fret or fuss,
For in twisted histories, we're all bound to trust!

Relationships in Thread

We stitch our lives with luck and cheer,
The needle's dance brings us near.
Sometimes we tangle, what a sight!
Like cats that wrestle late at night.

In laughter's bobbin, we loop and spin,
With every quirk, we find our win.
A patchwork tale of blunders bold,
Glimmers of warmth in threads of gold.

Each fabric scrap tells a different joke,
Like Auntie's socks that surely spoke.
With woven humor, our hearts all blend,
In this crazy quilt, we find a friend.

And when things fray, we simply grin,
For troubles counted are kites in the wind.
So here's to quirks that make us whole,
In this crazy fabric, we find our role.

The Quilt of Memory

In patches bright, our memories gleam,
Like grandma's quilt caught in a dream.
Each little square, a story spun,
A game of hide and seek—what fun!

There's a slice of cake, a puppy's bark,
A dance in the rain, we left our mark.
Stitched with laughter, tied with grace,
In every square, a familiar face.

Misplaced socks and missing keys,
We stitch our life with quirky ease.
A colorful patch, a snag or two,
But that's the charm in what we do.

So let's embrace this fabriced cheer,
In every thread, our tales appear.
With needle and thread, we claim our space,
In the quilt of life, we find our place.

Spun Together

In circles tight, we twirl and play,
Like yarn at dusk on a lazy day.
With every twist, we weave some fun,
And laugh as we dance, our lives undone.

The spools may scatter, the colors blend,
Each little hiccup, we call a trend.
A slippery knot or a loop gone wrong,
But we hum our tune, we sing along.

Our threads may tangle, but that's no crime,
For every mess just adds more rhyme.
We spin our stories, we share a thread,
In the fabric of life, together we tread.

So here's to the knots that keep us near,
In the fabric of friendship, let's share a cheer!
With a wink and a wink, let's dance and stumble,
In this joyful weave, together we jumble.

Tapestry of Tales

We weave our lives, a story grand,
With each bright thread passing through hand.
A little laugh, a twist of fate,
Our colorful stories, oh how they crate!

In fibers crossed, our secrets grow,
From silly yarns to laughter's flow.
Like awkward silences shared in glee,
These tangled threads set our spirits free.

A patch of blue for skies above,
Sprinkled with red from notes of love.
Each tale stitched with care and zest,
In this tapestry, we find our best.

So here's to the threads, both strong and bright,
In every tangle, there lies delight.
With laughter stitched in every seam,
We create a fabric that's more than a dream.

Stitched Stories

In a world where fabric's fate,
Every stitch holds quite the weight.
A seamstress whispers to her thread,
"Don't run away!" the fabric said.

Lopsided pockets, buttons lost,
They've journeyed far, but at what cost?
Each quirky patch, a tale to tell,
Of how that button liked to swell.

A quilt of memories, laughters sewn,
With patterns wild that we've outgrown.
Despite the flaws, we wear it well,
This patchwork's charm casts quite a spell.

So gather 'round for tales of old,
Of every thread, a story told.
In stitches we find joy and cheer,
Our fabric lives, forever near.

A Cord of Kinship

A knot for grandma, a twist for dad,
A family bound by chaos, not so bad.
Every misfit thread, a bond so strong,
In this wild tapestry, we all belong.

A cousin's sock, a missing mate,
Who wore it first? No need to debate!
With mismatched colors, we laugh and grow,
In every family blow, there's room for show.

When one falls short, we stitch it anew,
A safety net for me, and you.
Through tangled tales, love interweaves,
Our cord of kinship, one never leaves.

So here's to flaws and colors bright,
In laughter's fabric, we find our light.
Together we fashion quite the fleet,
Of memories cherished, and life so sweet.

Needle and Yarn

With pointy ends and tangles near,
A needle pricks a laugh, oh dear!
Yarn balls roll with antics grand,
As the cat plots a yarny stand.

The knots we make, a jumbled spree,
A tangled mess, just let it be!
A scarf that's shorter than a sleeve,
"Fashion, darling!" we just believe.

In every stitch, a giggle found,
As we knit together, happiness abound.
With colors clashing, style divine,
What's a faux pas? Just redefine!

So raise your needles, give a cheer,
For every yarn that brings us near.
In playful stitches, life is spun,
In laughter's weave, we've already won!

The Unity of Fabric

In a patchwork world where quirks unite,
Every fabric tells, a laugh at night.
Socks mismatched, yet proudly worn,
In this world of color, we are reborn.

Quilts of giggles, swatches of glee,
A fabric of memories, come see!
Each snip and snap a merry dance,
Let's stitch it up, let's take a chance.

We wear our flaws like badges bright,
Patterns of chaos, pure delight.
Fraying edges, oh what a sight,
In silly moments, we take flight.

So gather 'round, let's cut and sew,
With fabric crumbs, our laughter flows.
In the unity of fabric thralls,
We find the joy, that never falls.

www.ingramcontent.com/pod-product-compliance
Lightning Source LLC
Chambersburg PA
CBHW062109280426
43661CB00086B/378